HAL LEONARD

BASS METHOD

BY ED FRIEDLAND

SECOND EDITION

 Each track is recorded in stereo, with bass panned hard right. To remove the bass, adjust the balance control on your playback device.

All instruments performed by Ed Friedland.
Edited by Doug Downing

ISBN 978-0-7935-6381-4

CORPORATION
7777 W. BLUEMOUND RD. P.O. BOX 13819 MILWAUKEE, WI 53213

THE CHROMATIC WALKUP

 **TUNING NOTES**

TRACK 1

The **walkup** is a classic pattern used in rock, R&B, gospel, funk, blues, and many other styles. It starts on the root of a chord and uses a chromatic (half-step) motion to return to the root.

The simplest version of this is a one-measure pattern that drops from the root to the 6th and then moves back up.

The walkup can also drop down to the 3rd of the lower octave for a longer buildup.

The following walkup moves up to the octave. To get back to the starting note, it drops to the 3rd and goes up to the 5th. It jumps down a 7th in the middle of the pattern to finish back at the root. Notice where the shift happens.

TRACK 2

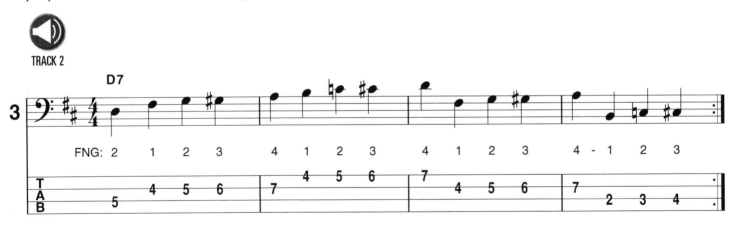

TIP: The pattern above is based on a universal fingering (one-finger-per-fret), so it's movable to any root, chord, or key. Try it on another root on the E or A string. (The shorter versions shown above are also movable.)

This extended version of the walkup alternates between low and high movement. It's a great way to keep the bass line interesting over a long section of one chord. Notice the shifts.

TRACK 3

The walkup can be played in any key, but the fingering does change in open position. Also, notice how the line has been modified at the end to bring it back to the E chord.

TRACK 4
SLOW/FAST

OPEN UP

Playing your notes short is called **staccato**. The little spaces in between each note gives the bass line a "pumping" feel. Staccato is indicated by a small dot (•) above the note.

Here's how it's done: Play the first note with either the index (i) or middle (m) finger. Before playing the next note, place the alternate finger on the string and stop its vibration. Then play the next note. Practice this slowly first, then gradually increase the tempo.

If playing pick style, use your left hand to stop the string's vibration.

This classic variation on the chromatic walkup is known as the "double stroke." Make each note even and consistent. It's written staccato, but also experiment with different note lengths. Start on the 4th finger using the 1-2-4 fingering system, but switch to one-finger-per-fret (OFPF) in measure 3. When you repeat, use the 1st finger to play the low C.

TRACK 5
SLOW/FAST

DOUBLE UP

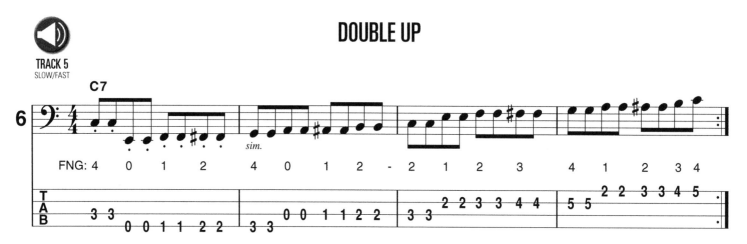

Here are two ways of notating a syncopated eighth-note rhythm. They sound identical, but the untied version is less confusing to the eye.

USING TIES

COUNT: 1   +   (2)   +

UNTIED

COUNT: 1   +   (2)   +

TRACK 6

REZ - Q

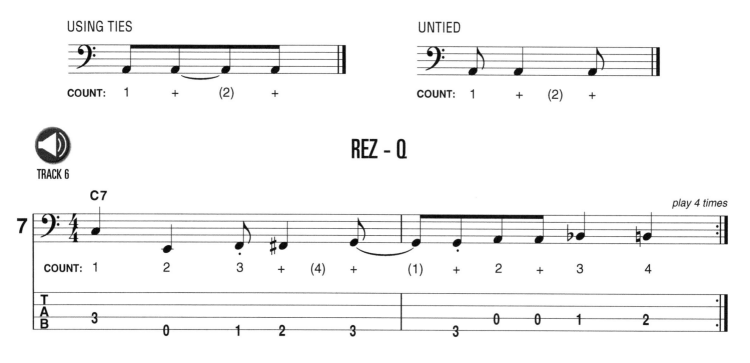

This moves the walkup through several chord changes. Slowly count your way through the extended syncopation in measures 6 and 7.

SIXTEENTH NOTES

Sixteenth notes break each quarter note into four equal subdivisions. They are counted, "1-ee-and-uh, 2-ee-and-uh," etc. In groups, sixteenth notes are written with a double beam connecting them. Separately, they have a double "flag."

COUNT: 1 e + a 2 e + a 3 e + a 4 e + a

Practice sixteenths slowly, aiming for consistent volume and tone. Once you are comfortable, use a metronome clicking quarter notes to gauge your rhythmic accuracy.

Fingerstyle, keep alternating between index (i) and middle (m) fingers. Pick style, observe the downstroke (⊓) and upstroke (∨) indications shown.

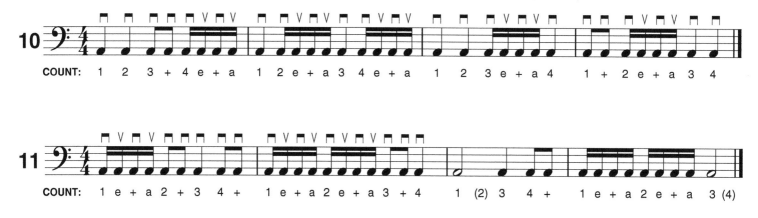

10

COUNT: 1   2   3 + 4 e + a   1   2 e + a 3   4 e + a   1   2   3 e + a 4   1 + 2 e + a 3   4

11

COUNT: 1 e + a 2 + 3   4 +   1 e + a 2 e + a 3 + 4   1 (2) 3   4 +   1 e + a 2 e + a 3 (4)

The quarter note can be broken up many ways using sixteenths. When an eighth and two sixteenths are combined, it is helpful at first to count the silent sixteenth ("ee") during the eighth note.

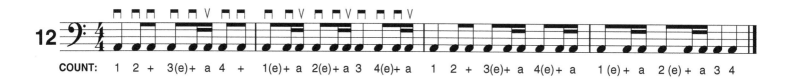

12

COUNT: 1   2 + 3(e)+ a 4 +   1(e)+ a 2(e)+ a 3   4(e)+ a   1   2 + 3(e)+ a 4(e)+ a   1 (e)+ a 2 (e)+ a 3   4

The same is true for two sixteenths and an eighth.

13

COUNT: 1   2 e +(a) 3   4   1 e +(a) 2   3 e +(a) 4   1 + 2 e +(a) 3   4 +   1 + 2 e +(a) 3 e +(a) 4

ONE DROP

DADA DADAT

JOG WHEEL

SIXTEENTH RESTS

Sixteenth rests take up the same space as sixteenth notes. They look similar to eighth rests, but they have a double flag (instead of a single) to match the double flag of a sixteenth note.

To play sixteenth rests, you'll need to stop the string from vibrating. Use the same technique you used to play staccato: first play a note with either the index (i) or middle (m) finger; then place the alternate finger on the string and stop the vibration. If playing pickstyle, use your left hand to mute the string (observe the picking indications shown).

Now count for yourself; do it slowly.

Here is an example that combines sixteenth-note rhythms and rests with the C major scale.

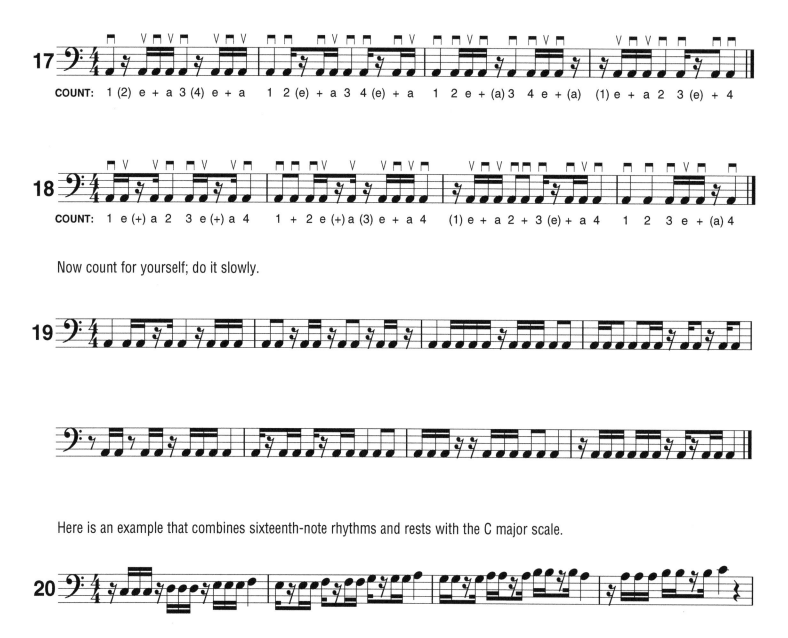

Notice the sixteenth-note **anticipation** in the last measure; the E is played slightly ahead of the beat.

LAYIN' BACK

TRACK 12

Keep track of the missing downbeats; it will help you hit the sixteenth-note offbeats with greater assurance.

NAZZ - T

TRACK 13

PLUTONIC

TRACK 14
SLOW/FAST

FUNKY SIXTEENTH-NOTE SYNCOPATION

Syncopated sixteenth notes are the essence of funk, Latin, and rock music. Though they are challenging to look at, the rhythms are very familiar to the ear. The key is learning to recognize the sound that matches the picture.

This rhythm uses a **dotted eighth note** and a sixteenth. Remember that a *dot* equals one half of whatever value it is placed after. So a dotted eighth note equals the value of one eighth plus a sixteenth (or three sixteenths).

An easy way to remember this rhythm is to give it a name that sounds like it. Call it "oo-(ka-chu)-bop."

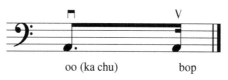

oo (ka chu)   bop

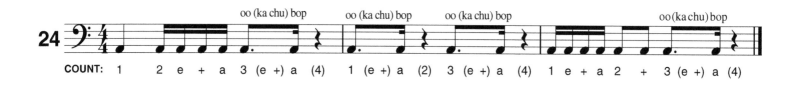

24

COUNT: 1 2 e + a 3 (e +) a (4) 1 (e +) a (2) 3 (e +) a (4) 1 e + a 2 + 3 (e +) a (4)

25

COUNT: 1 + 2(e+)a 3 e + a 4 1 + 2(e+)a 3(e+)a 4

TRACK 15
SLOW/FAST

OOKACHU WHA?

FNG: 1   0 4 4   1   1 4 1   0 4

A version of "ookachubop" uses a **dotted eighth rest** and a sixteenth note. Say the "ookachu" silently; it will help you play it correctly. This rhythm can be used alone as an upbeat syncopation, or in front of another note as a "pickup" beat.

GROOVE

TRACK 16
SLOW/FAST

Call this new rhythm "check-on-dat."

31

COUNT: 1 e (+) a 2 (e+) a 3 + 4

COMBO

TRACK 17

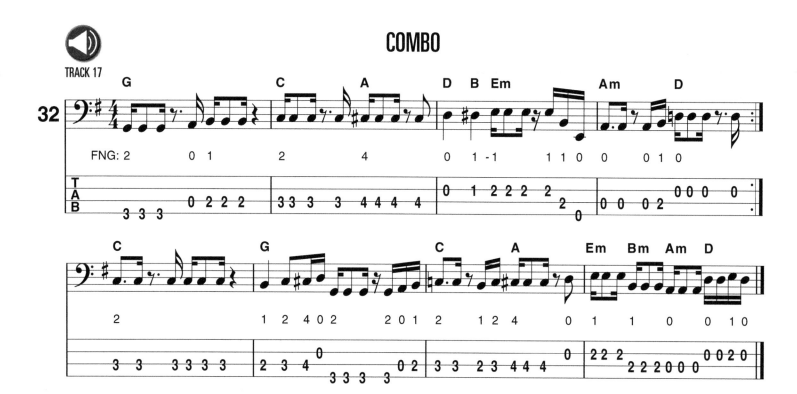

This next rhythm is similar to "check on dat"; it hits on the "e" and "a" of the beat. Call it "(chk) got - dot"; the (chk) is spoken as a place marker but not played.

33

COUNT: (1) e (+) a (2)e(+) a 3 + 4   1(e+)a (2e)+ a (3) e (+) a 4   1 + 2 e + a (3) e (+) a (4)

34

COUNT: (1) e (+) a 2   (3) e (+) a 4 (e) + a   1 (e +) a 2   +   3 e + a (4) e (+) a

MINOR GLITCH

This rhythm hits on the downbeat and the "e." A good name for it is "chick-en."

A variation of "chick-en" uses a rest on the downbeat, making the "chick" silent.

38

COUNT: 1   (2) e (+a) 3   (4) e (+a) 1   +   (2 e +)a   3 (e +) a   (4) e (+a) 1   +   (2) e (+a) 3 e (+) a 4

It's interesting to combine the "names" for different rhythms. Creating rhythmic "sentences" like this can help you remember tricky rhythms and play them with assurance. When you first look through this example, see how many rhythm "names" you can identify.

DO IT NOW

TRACK 19

When taking the repeat back to measure 1, play the low G with the first finger. Switch back to open when you play the A.

SOUL GROOVE

TRACK 20
SLOW/FAST

D - TROIT

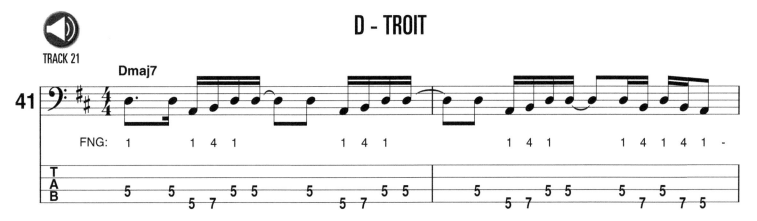

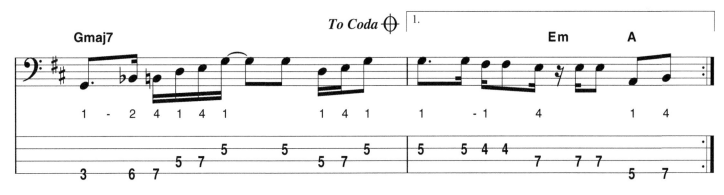

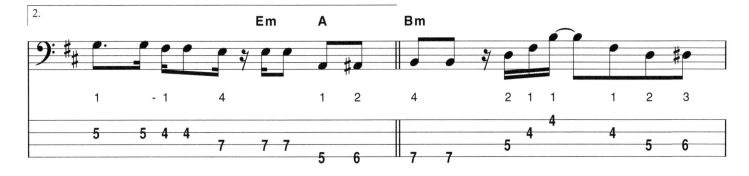

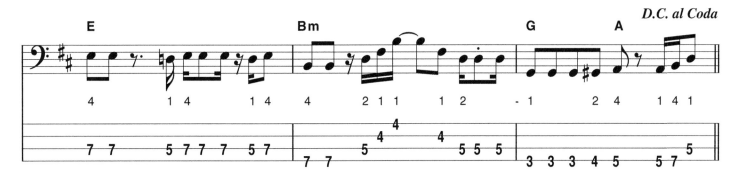

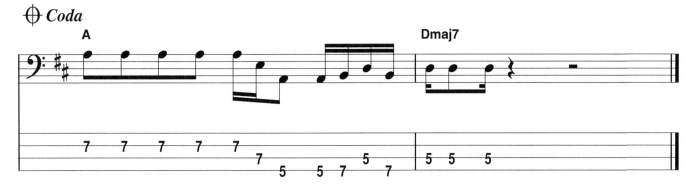

SEVENTH CHORDS

Seventh chords are four-note structures that contain the familiar major and minor triads—root, 3rd, and 5th—plus one more note, the 7th. There are several types of seventh chord; we'll look at the three most common.

MAJOR SEVENTH

The major seventh chord is built 1-3-5-7. The chord symbol is written as "maj7," though some books write it as "M7" or "Δ7." There is a universal fingering for the major seventh chord that allows you to play it in any key.

When you practice these arpeggios, become familiar with the specific note names that "spell" each chord. Try the universal fingering, as well as open fingerings where indicated.

FLOATY

TRACK 22

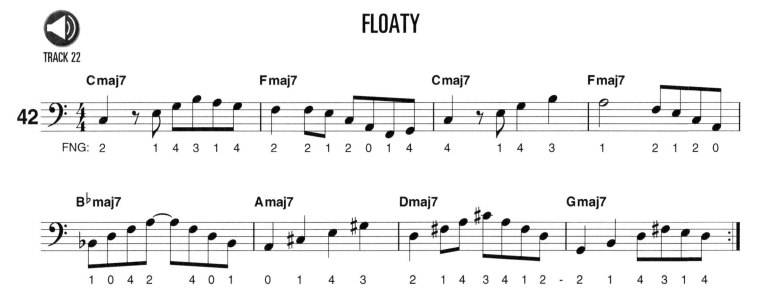

The tablature will help you find the best positions for this example, but experiment with other ways to play it.

VANILLA

TRACK 23

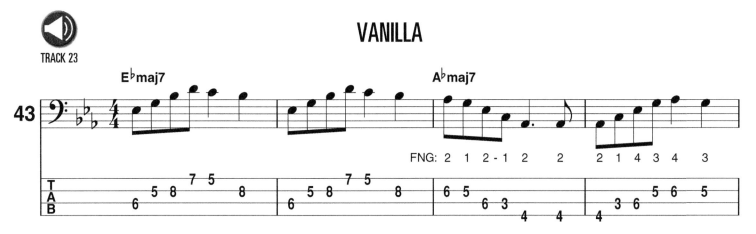

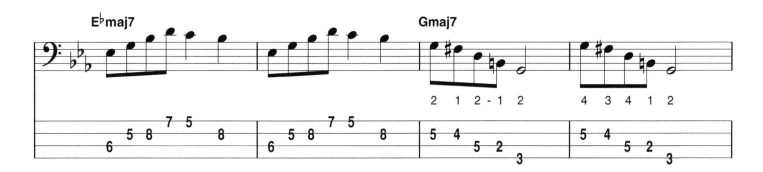

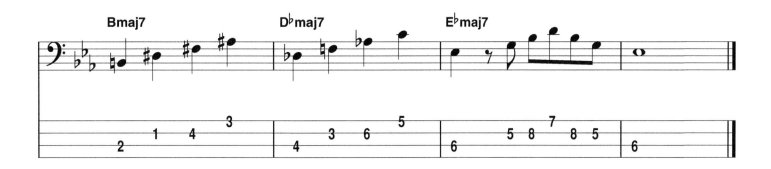

DOMINANT SEVENTH

Dominant seventh chords are also known simply as "7" chords, as in "G7" or "A7."

They are built 1-3-5-♭7, and the universal fingering is 2-1-4-2.

Remember to learn the names of the notes in each chord, and find alternate fingerings. Practice the universal fingering, as well as open fingerings, where indicated.

The blues is always full of dominant seventh chords; here is a classic example of how to use the arpeggio to create a bass line.

MINOR SEVENTH

Minor seventh chords are built 1-♭3-5-♭7. They can be written "m7" as in "Am7" (or "min7" as in "Amin7").

There are two universal fingerings for a minor seventh chord; they are best illustrated with Am7.

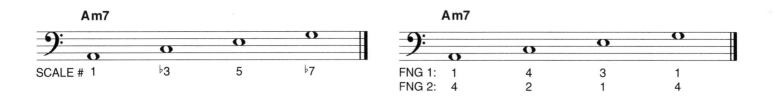

Say the note names aloud as you play each arpeggio. Try both universal fingerings, and open fingerings where indicated.

LITTLE M

This piece is played with a shuffle, or swing, feel. Be sure to play the eighth notes "unevenly"—i.e., as if they were the first and third notes of a triplet. The shuffle indication (♫ = ♩♪) tells you this.

SHUFFLIN'

These examples combine the different seventh chords.

MIDDLE MAN

ON THE VERGE

SLIDES

Sliding into a note is a great way to give your bass line personality. It can sound relaxed and loose, or create a dramatic effect. When sliding from one note to another, slightly relax the pressure on the slide finger to avoid making the fret sound too pronounced. Practice sliding with different fingers, at various speeds, and different distances. If a slide has a "slur" marking above it, only the first note is plucked; the second note is simply slid into.

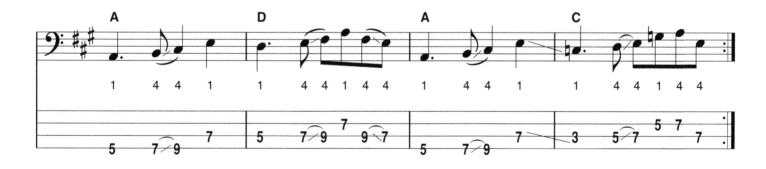

SLIPPIN' & SLIDIN'

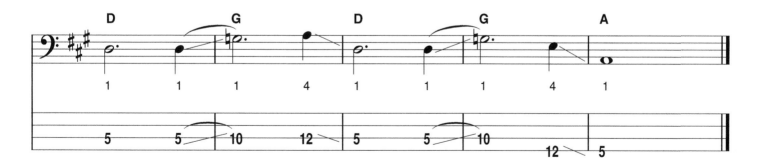

MINOR PENTATONIC

Pentatonic scales are five-note structures that are widely used in all styles of music. The **minor pentatonic** scale is built 1-♭3-4-5-♭7-8 (the octave is not counted as a separate note; hence the name penta-tonic).

There are two universal fingerings. The first is based on the minor scale position and uses one finger per fret; the second uses the 1-2-4 fingering system and starts on the 4th finger, shifting up between scale degrees 4 and 5.

A MINOR PENTATONIC

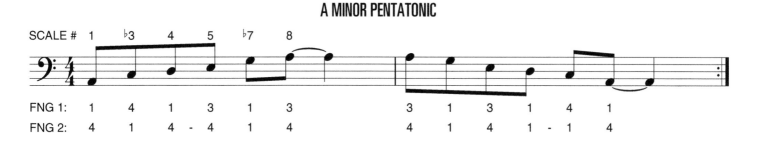

Here are the most common keys for the minor pentatonic scale. E minor pentatonic is in open position and has a unique fingering; the rest use the universal fingerings shown above. Optional open position fingerings are also indicated in some cases.

E MINOR PENT.   B MINOR PENT.

F# MINOR PENT.   C# MINOR PENT.

G# MINOR PENT.   D MINOR PENT.

G MINOR PENT.   C MINOR PENT.

F MINOR PENT.   B♭ MINOR PENT.

The minor pentatonic scale works well when you have to "jam" or improvise on one chord. This example shows you how to play up and down the scale in G and C.

VENTURE FORTH

TRACK 31
SLOW/FAST

This example uses a repetitive minor pentatonic idea or "lick" and moves it around to match the chord changes.

DEJA VIEW

TRACK 32

HAMMER-ONS & PULL-OFFS

Two adjacent notes on the same string can be played with one pluck of the finger using a **hammer-on** or a **pull-off**. Play a lower note with the 1st finger, and then "hammer on" to the higher note with the 4th finger. Reverse this action by playing a higher note with the 4th finger, and then "pull off" to the 1st. These articulations are indicated with a slur marking.

TRACK 33

TRACK 34
SLOW/FAST

HAMMER HEAD

Here is a two-octave fingering for E minor pentatonic. It uses slides while shifting positions. Notice the slides are in different locations going up and down.

The chord progression of this example follows the notes of the E minor pentatonic scale, a common approach in rock song-writing.

TRACK 35

X-TENDER

MAJOR PENTATONIC

The **major pentatonic** scale is also widely used in many styles of music. It is built 1-2-3-5-6-8. There are two universal fingerings. The first follows the major scale position using OFPF; the second uses the 1-2-4 fingering system and starts on the 1st finger, shifting up the string between scale degrees 2 and 3.

C MAJOR PENTATONIC

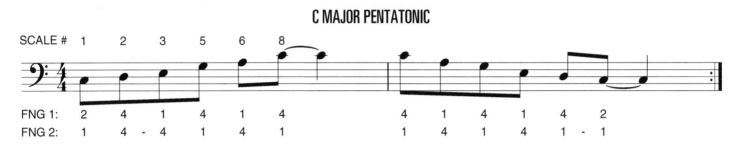

SCALE #	1	2	3	5	6	8		4	1	4	1	4	2
FNG 1:	2	4	1	4	1	4		4	1	4	1	4	2
FNG 2:	1	4	- 4	1	4	1		1	4	1	4	1	- 1

Here are the other common keys for the major pentatonic scale. They can all use the two universal fingerings, except for E and F, which are in open position. G, A, and B♭ are marked with optional open-position fingerings.

G MAJOR PENT.
FNG: 2 0 1 0 1 0

D MAJOR PENT.

A MAJOR PENT.
FNG: 0 1 4 1 4 1

E MAJOR PENT.
0 1 4 1 4 1

B MAJOR PENT.

F MAJOR PENT.
FNG: 1 4 0 4 0 4

B♭ MAJOR PENT.
FNG: 1 4 0 4 0 4

E♭ MAJOR PENT.

A♭ MAJOR PENT.

D♭ MAJOR PENT.

JUST LIKE MY GIRL

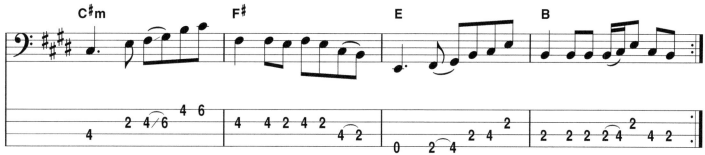

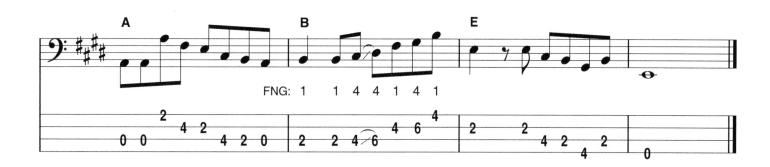

N'AWLINS BEAT

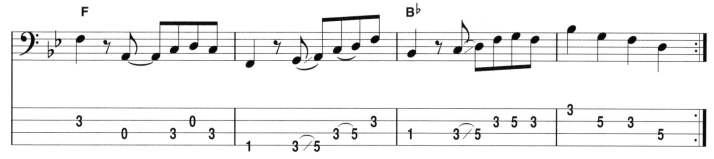

PLAYING OFF CHORD SYMBOLS

While most of what you've learned so far has been written out for you, the bassist is often called upon to create his or her own part or line based on a series of chord symbols. Fortunately, it is fairly simple to create solid, functional bass lines that outline a chord progression using the information you already have at your disposal.

The first priority of a good bass line is to establish the **root motion**—that is, movement from one chord to the next. By using the rhythmic feel of the song and playing the root of each new chord, you can create a perfectly usable bass line that, while not exotic, is often the best thing to play. You'll usually have several possible locations to choose for each root—avoid making jumps bigger than an octave from one root to another.

JUST ROOTS

TRACK 38

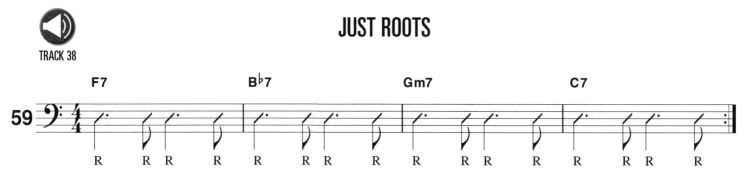

Here is the same chord progression using a steady eighth-note rhythm.

ROOTS & 8THS

TRACK 39

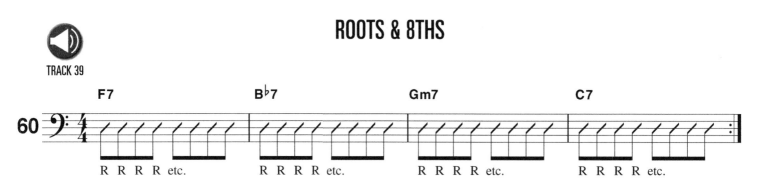

The **octave** is still the root of the chord, but it gives the line a feeling of movement. You can start on the lower root and use the higher octave, or you can reverse this and start on the higher octave and use the low root for movement.

JUMPING OCTAVES

TRACK 40

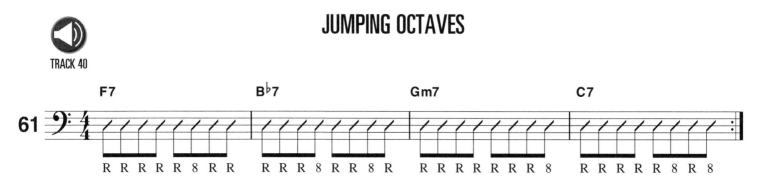

TIP: When playing octaves fingerstyle, it's often easiest to use a "split fingering": middle finger (m) on the higher string and index (i) on the lower. When alternating fingers on a single string with occasional octave jumps, use your middle finger to jump up to the octave, and your index finger to jump down.

Play your own bass line to this chord progression. Using the suggested rhythm, play roots and octaves.

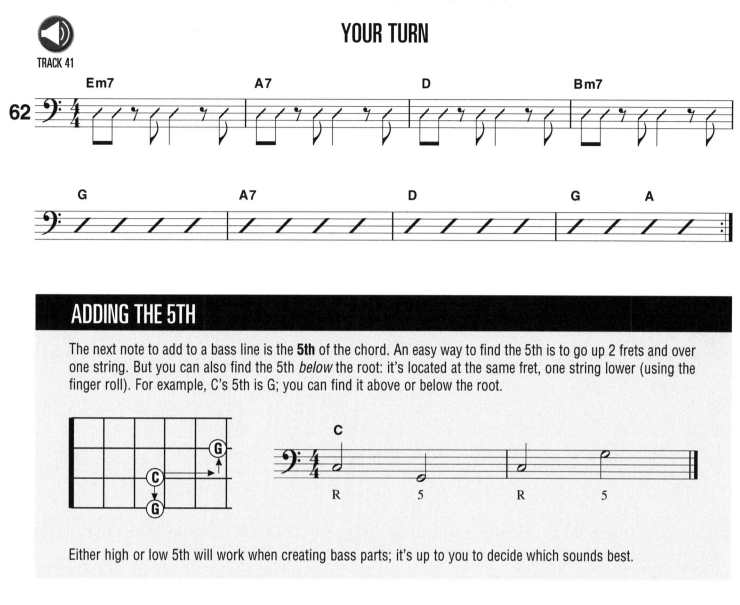

YOUR TURN

ADDING THE 5TH

The next note to add to a bass line is the **5th** of the chord. An easy way to find the 5th is to go up 2 frets and over one string. But you can also find the 5th *below* the root: it's located at the same fret, one string lower (using the finger roll). For example, C's 5th is G; you can find it above or below the root.

Either high or low 5th will work when creating bass parts; it's up to you to decide which sounds best.

Notice how smooth transitions from one chord to the next can create direction in a line. In this progression, starting on the higher F gives you the option of playing the low 5th, which flows easily into the lower Bb; the high 5th of Bb moves nicely into the higher G, and so on. It's important to keep this type of close movement in mind when creating your own bass part.

USE THE 5

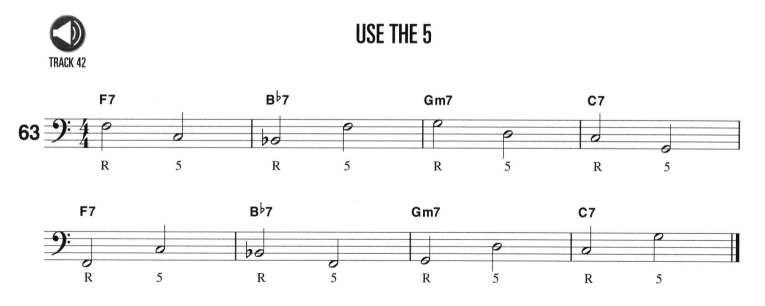

Create your own part using the steady eighth-note rhythm. You can play it through once using the lower root choices, and the next time with the higher ones.

5 BY 8

TRACK 43

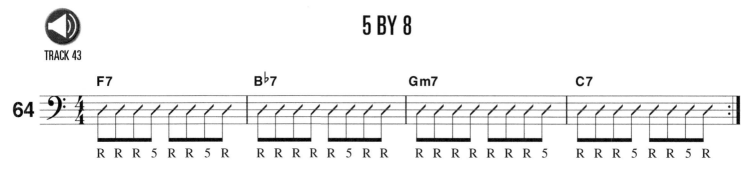

Roots, 5ths, and octaves outline the basic structure of any chord; they are safe choices that work with any chord type. This time, use the root, 5th, and octave together to create a line. Remember that you can start on a low root and move up to the octave, or you can start on a high root and move down to a low octave.

ROOT-5-8

TRACK 44

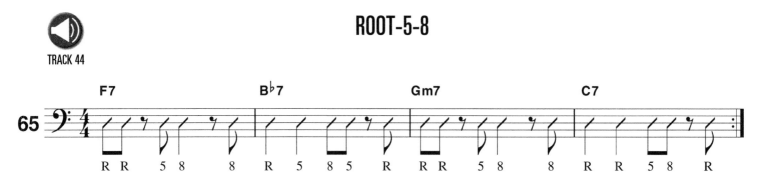

Create your own bass line to this progression using roots, 5ths, and octaves. Use the indicated rhythm, and alternate the line from octave to root on one chord, root to octave on the next. Then see what variations you can find.

YOU GOT IT

TRACK 45

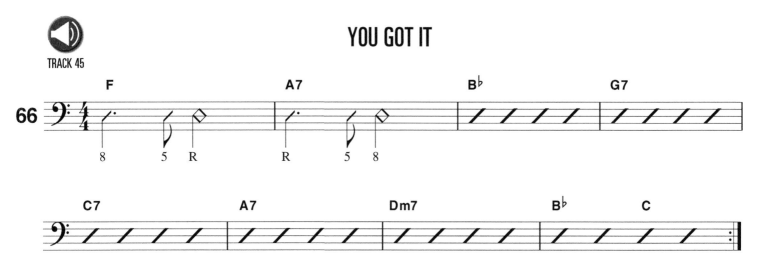

CHROMATIC APPROACH

The root, 5th, and octave are **target notes**; you aim for the root on the downbeat of a new chord, while the 5th and octave are two notes that allow for movement during the measure without interfering with the chord type. To create even more movement in the bass line, we add **approach notes**—notes that *lead into* a target note.

Chromatic approach notes lead into the target note by a half step (one fret). They can approach the target from above or below. Notice how this bass line uses a chromatic approach (chr) to lead into the root of each new chord. In measures 3 and 4, a "chr" is also used to lead into the 5th, adding more movement to the line.

When choosing your chromatic approach notes, remember to try them from above *and* below the target note.

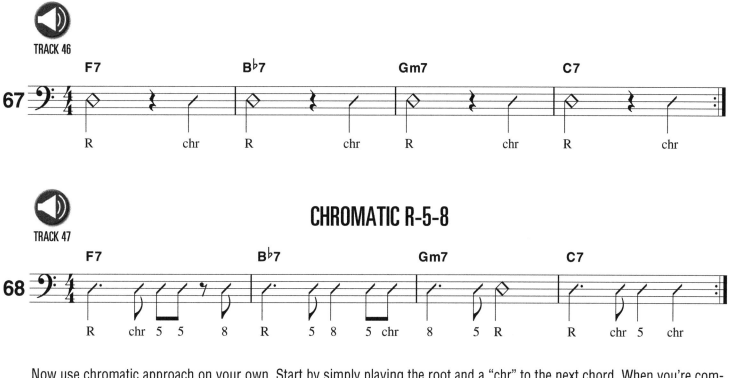

Now use chromatic approach on your own. Start by simply playing the root and a "chr" to the next chord. When you're comfortable with the progression, add the 5th of each chord. Then use "chr" to lead into those 5ths. Any of the rhythms from previous examples will work; start simply, and then experiment.

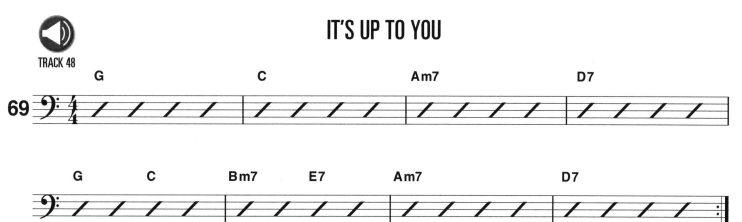

SCALE APPROACH

Scale approach uses the adjacent scale tone (from above or below) to approach the target note. Use the scale of the *new* target chord. Most of the time, scale approach is a whole step (2 frets). There are, however, instances where the scale tone may be a half step away from the target—for example, when approaching a major chord from below. It doesn't matter whether you call it scale or chromatic approach; just use it.

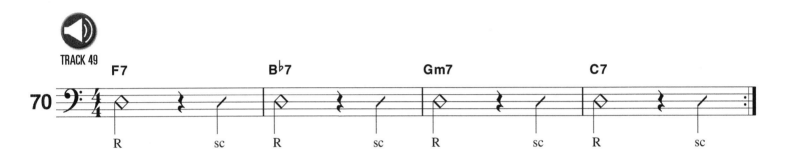

TIP: When approaching a dominant seventh chord (e.g., A7) from below, use a ♭7 scale degree to match the chord.

TRACK 49

70

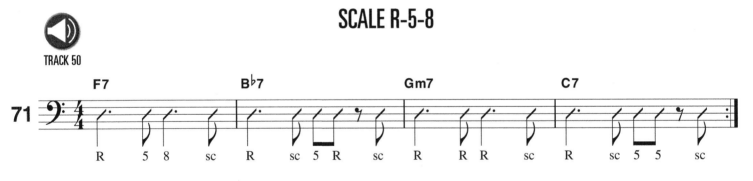

This uses "sc" to the 5th on the B♭7 and C7. Once you are comfortable with this version, look for other ways to use "sc" with this progression.

SCALE R-5-8

TRACK 50

71

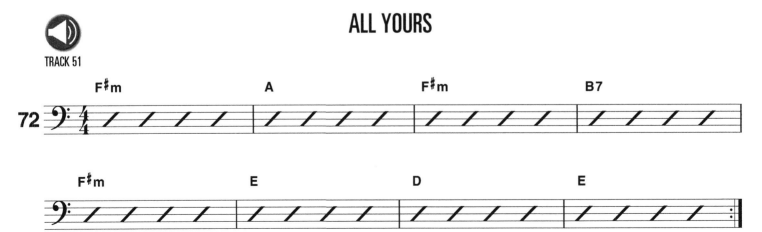

Applying any rhythm previously played, use scale approach to move from one chord to the next. Then try adding the 5th and approaching it when you choose. (Tip: For minor chords, remember to use a ♭6 when approaching the 5th.)

ALL YOURS

TRACK 51

72

DOMINANT APPROACH

Dominant approach uses the 5th of the target note. Many chord progressions are built with dominant root motion, which is when the root motion resolves to a new chord from its 5th. In those cases, using a dominant approach simply outlines the existing root motion. Using "dom" between chords that do *not* have a dominant root motion creates a very strong movement.

TRACK 52

It's tricky at first to grasp using the "dom" of the 5th. This line illustrates the concept effectively. (Hint: It's basically scale degree 2 of the chord.)

DOMINANT TO THE 5TH

TRACK 53

Now use dominant approach on your own. You can add the "dom" that leads into the 5th anytime you want. When the root motion is already dominant, just use the root.

YOU GO, HUGO

TRACK 54

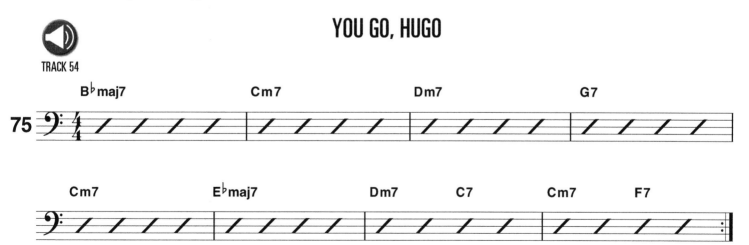

USING TRIADS TO CREATE BASS LINES

Triads can be used to build bass lines that clearly state the chord progression. Used in conjunction with the root-5-8 and various approach notes, you have a very complete set of tools to construct an interesting and functional bass part.

The first step is to recognize which *type* of triad the chord symbol indicates. Here are the five basic chord structures you've learned so far. Major and minor triads are easy to grasp; major seventh and dominant seventh chords have major triads as their foundation, while the minor seventh chord contains a minor triad.

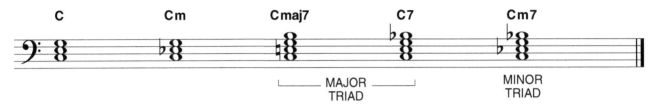

Here is an example of using triads with an approach note to each new chord. Using a quarter-note rhythm, we wind up with a classic walking bass line in a jazz style.

WALKING TRIADS

TRACK 55
SLOW/FAST

Now it's your turn to walk through the "changes." Stick to triads only at first. You can vary your line by playing the chord tones in a different order and direction.

WALK THIS WAY

TRACK 56

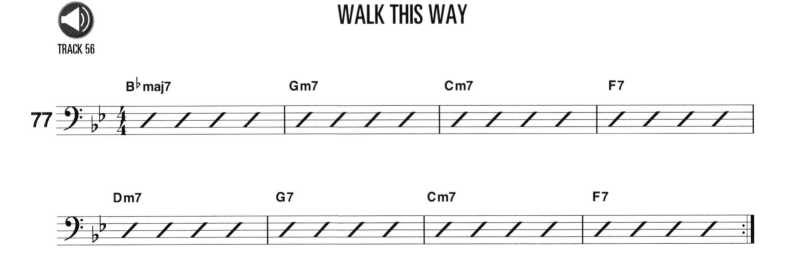

It is possible to "bounce around" within the triad—notice that the F triad below changes directions. The second half is open for you to make your own choices; make sure you are familiar with each triad before playing.

SIMPLE TRIADS

TRACK 57

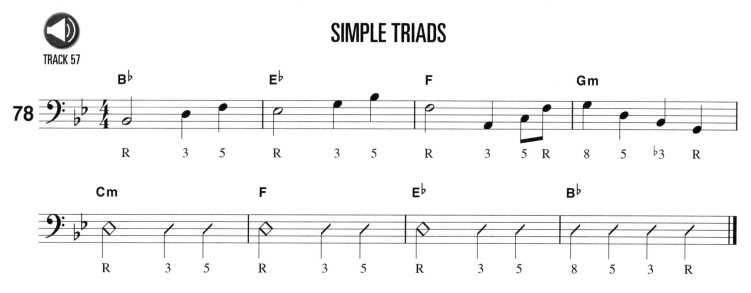

Once you're comfortable with a chord progression, try adding approach notes on beat 4. Remember: you have three ways of approaching a target note: by half step (1 fret), whole step (2 frets), or by 5th. Play the triad for the first three beats of each measure, but focus your attention on the upcoming chord, and play around with different approaches to its root.

ON YOUR OWN

TRACK 58

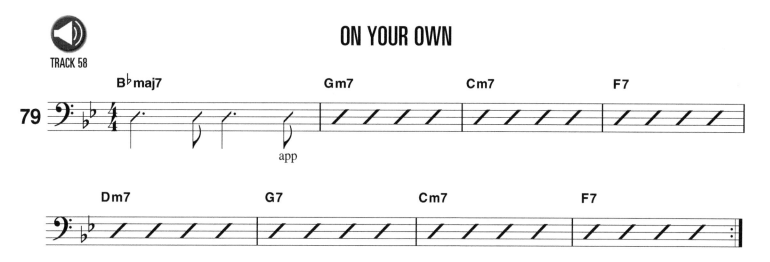

Here's the same chord progression as example 76, played with a dotted quarter/eighth note rhythm. Notice the different ways the triad gets placed in the measure. Also notice the approach notes—nearly all of them are also chord tones! (Can you spot the one that isn't?)

TRIADS & DOTTED QUARTERS

TRACK 59

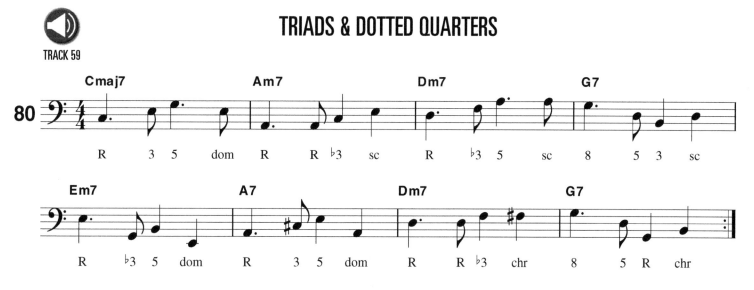

Create your own bass line for this song; use all the methods you've learned so far. Any rhythm will work.

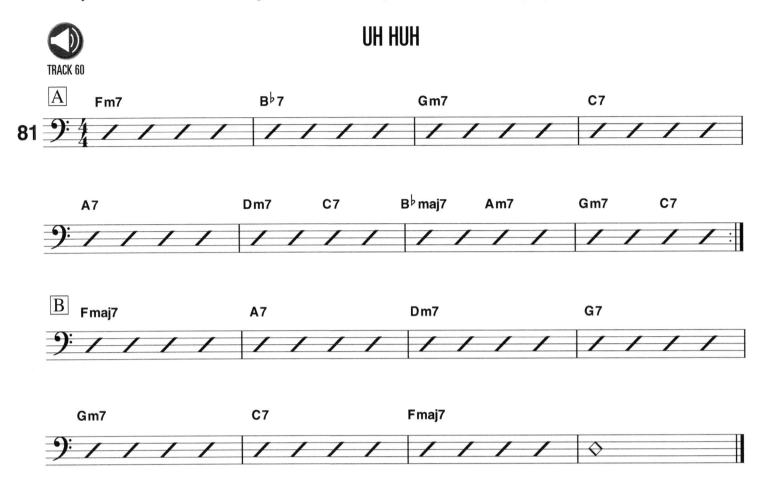

UH HUH

TRACK 60

LOCKING IN TO THE GROOVE

A **groove** is any particular rhythmic idea that forms the basis of a song. When bass and drums play together, they need to connect their parts so that it feels like one unified beat. The term "locking in to the groove" is used to describe this phenomenon. To lock in, the bassist and drummer must listen to each other's part and find a shared sense of where the groove is, so they can play together. One way that bassists and drummers connect is by matching the bass line with the kick drum. Examples A and B are two common rhythms you've worked with. Examine the matching drum part, and see how the bass line "hooks up" with the beat.

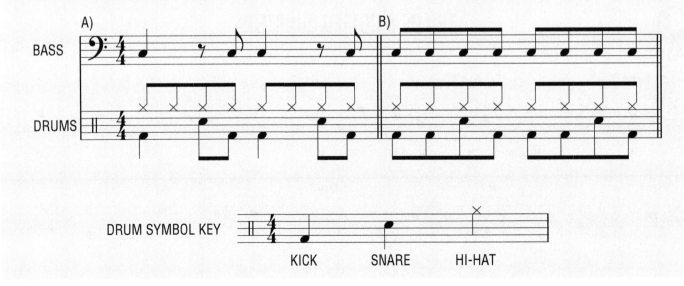

Here are six different rhythms, or grooves. Learn each, then apply it to the chord—in this case, C7. Start by playing only the root; once you've locked in with the groove, see what other notes you can play. Although there are many note choices available, you're not obligated to play them all. However, as a bassist, you are obligated to maintain the groove.

GROOVE JAM

TRACK 61

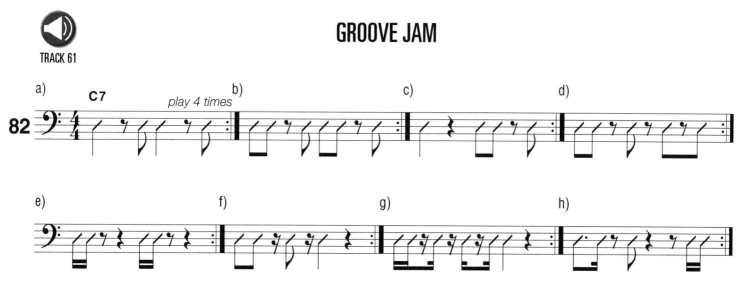

The grooves for the A and B sections are indicated. Use them as the basis for your line. Start with simple ideas that match the rhythm. As you listen more closely, you'll find it is possible to vary your line within the basic feel and still keep the groove intact. Experiment with different note choices; use root-5-8, chord tones, and different approach notes.

TIME 2 GROOVE

TRACK 62

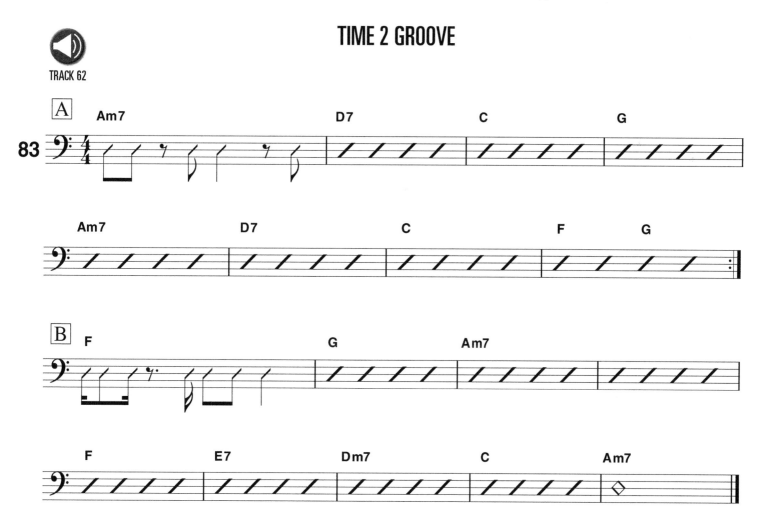

SLAP FUNK

The slap funk style started in the late 1960s and is still one of the most popular techniques that bassists use. The two essential elements of the technique are **slapping** the strings (with the thumb) and **popping** them (with the index and middle fingers).

THE SLAP

Keep the thumb parallel with the string—using the bony knob of your thumb knuckle for the striking surface, hit the string at the end of the fingerboard. Use a twist-like motion in the wrist, and pivot the forearm from the elbow to "whip" the thumb on and off the string. Make sure the thumb "recoils" off the string, allowing it to ring.

TIP: Round wound strings are best for slap funk. Medium to low string height allows the bass to respond to the thumb slap. You don't want to hit the string too hard; it's wasted energy, and it chokes the sound of the note.

Keep the right arm and shoulder loose and relaxed; tension in these areas greatly decreases how funky you can get!

Start by slapping the open strings. Strive for consistent volume and tone for each note, and from string to string. Mute the open strings with the left hand—laying your fingers flat across the strings—in between slaps, but give the note its full value. The slap will be notated using the letter "T" for thumb.

TRACK 63

Now practice switching strings; remember to keep the thumb parallel with the string for better accuracy.

This example requires you to slap up the E and A strings.

SLAP THIS

TRACK 64

This example takes you up a two-octave E minor pentatonic scale, a very common structure in slap funk. Strive for consistent volume from string to string.

PENT UP

TRACK 65

THE POP

The pop is achieved by pulling the string with the index or middle finger away from the neck, letting it snap back onto the frets. Make a loose fist with your right hand. Let the thumb come to rest against the E string, parallel as if you were going to slap it. Let your index finger naturally fall in between the D and G string, and the middle finger curl under the G. Pull from the side of the finger. Don't get "caught up" in the string; use just enough to pull the string lightly. Too much pull makes the pop louder than needed, and can cause broken strings.

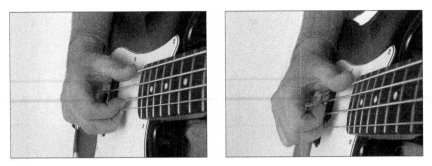

Although it is possible to slap or pop any string, for the most part, you will be slapping the E and A strings and popping the D and G. It works best to dedicate the index (1st) finger to popping the D string and the middle (2nd) finger to the G.

🔊 **TRACK 66**

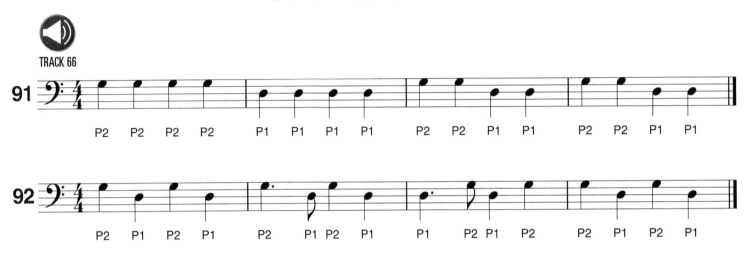

COMBINING SLAP AND POP

Slap the string, prepare to pop

Combining slap and pop into a smooth, two-piece movement is the next step. When you slap the string, move your finger into position for the pop. Let the thumb recoil from the slap without moving your hand away from the string, then slip the pop finger under the string and pull/release.

After slap, pop the string

🔊 **TRACK 67**

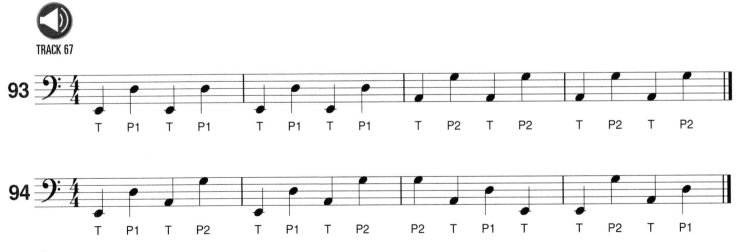

The octave is a very common part of slap funk. Practice playing these octaves with alternating slap and pop.

When play the octave C's, try letting the tip of your index finger mute the low E string.

OCTAVE SLAP

TRACK 68
SLOW/FAST

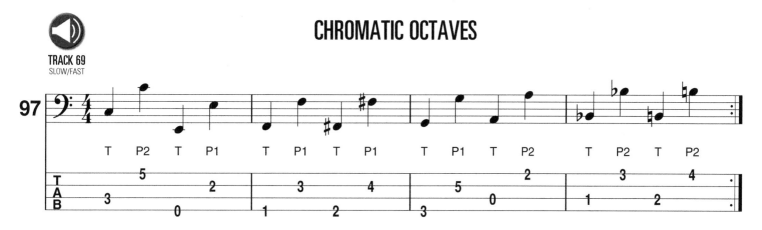

This exercise moves the slap/pop octave around the fingerboard. As usual, play the octave with the 1st and 4th fingers (left hand), but when you play the open E and A strings, use the 2nd finger for their octaves.

CHROMATIC OCTAVES

TRACK 69
SLOW/FAST

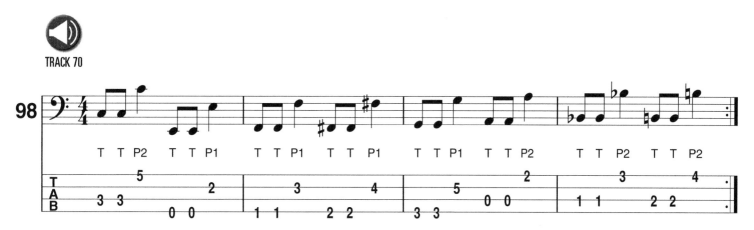

This rhythmic variation helps develop thumb control.

TRACK 70

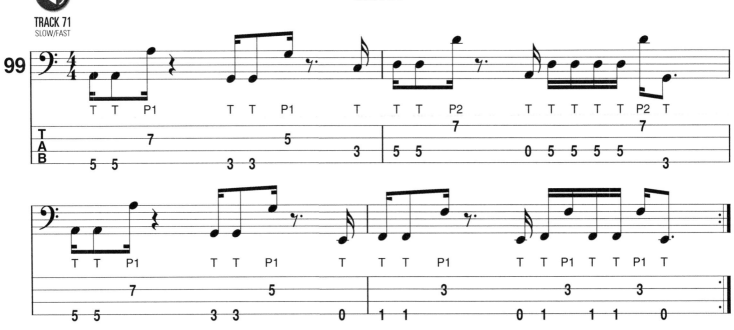

GRITTY

THE PRESSURE ROLL

The hammer-on is a technique you already know that's used often in slap funk. Sometimes, it's necessary to set up a hammer-on with the use of a **pressure roll** across the strings. Play a low G with the tip of the 1st finger as usual. Now *roll* the pressure used to push the string down, across to the D string, without dropping the tip of the fin-

Playing with tip

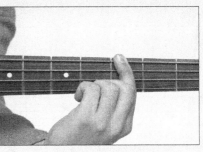

Pressure roll

ger; you'll play the F on the 3rd fret, D string with the bottom part of the 1st finger. This pressure roll allows you to smoothly jump across the strings between slap and pop.

Now use the pressure roll to set up the hammer-ons (indicated with a slur) from the 1st finger to the 4th.

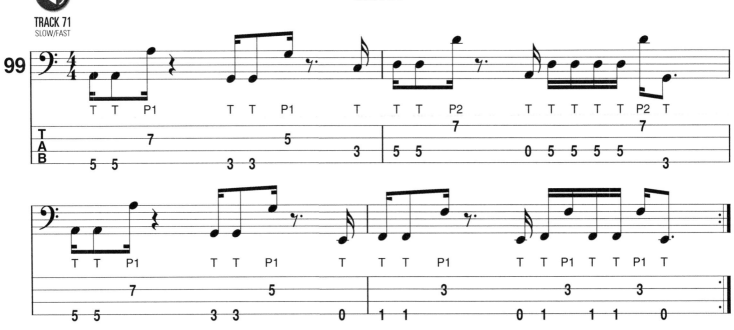

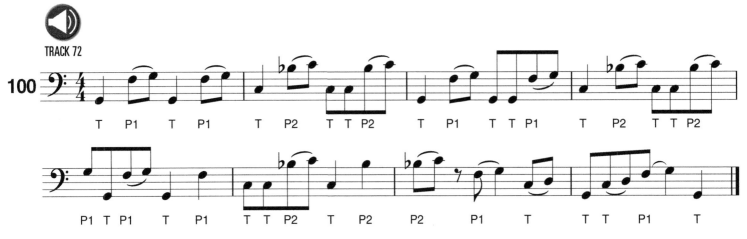

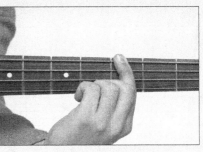

This example uses a pull-off as well as the hammer-on.

DEAD NOTES

Dead notes are an important part of the slap funk style. By not pushing the string all the way down to the fretboard (in the left hand), you produce a note that is not a true pitch. Slapping or popping these notes creates a unique percussive effect that blends in well.

DEAD END

The A section requires you to create your own bass line from the chord symbols and rhythm, while the B section has a specific slap funk line to play. It may take some practice to get comfortable switching from fingerstyle to slap; make sure you stay aware of the switch-over point in the song. The last two measures of the coda are played fingerstyle.

KEEP IT TOGETHER

TRACK 75

This one is a busy sixteenth-note tune with some technical challenges. Be sure to keep your tempo consistent.

IT'S AN EYEFUL!

TRACK 76

105

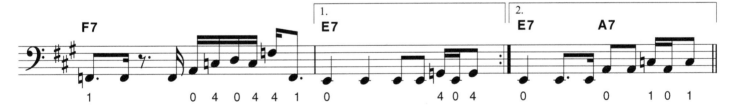

HAL LEONARD
BASS METHOD

METHOD BOOKS

by Ed Friedland

BOOK 1

Book 1 teaches: tuning; playing position; musical symbols; notes within the first five frets; common bass lines, patterns and rhythms; rhythms through eighth notes; playing tips and techniques; more than 100 great songs, riffs and examples; and more! The audio includes 44 full-band tracks for demonstration or play-along.
00695067 Book Only.................................. $7.99
00695068 Book/Online Audio.............................. $12.99

BOOK 2

Book 2 continues where Book 1 left off and teaches: the box shape; moveable boxes; notes in fifth position; major and minor scales; the classic blues line; the shuffle rhythm; tablature; and more!
00695069 Book Only.................................. $7.99
00695070 Book/Online Audio.............................. $12.99

BOOK 3

With the third book, progressing students will learn more great songs, riffs and examples; sixteenth notes; playing off chord symbols; slap and pop techniques; hammer-ons and pull-offs; playing different styles and grooves; and more.
00695071 Book Only.................................. $7.99
00695072 Book/Online Audio.............................. $12.99

COMPOSITE

This money-saving edition contains Books 1, 2 and 3.
00695073 Book Only.................................. $17.99
00695074 Book/Online Audio.............................. $24.99

DVD

Play your favorite songs in no time with this DVD! Covers: tuning, notes in first through third position, rhythms through eighth notes, fingerstyle and pick playing, 4/4 and 3/4 time, and more! Includes 6 full songs and on-screen music notation. 68 minutes.
00695849 DVD....................................... $19.95

BASS FOR KIDS
by Chad Johnson

Bass for Kids is a fun, easy course that teaches children to play bass guitar faster than ever before. Popular songs such as "Crazy Train," "Every Breath You Take," "A Hard Day's Night" and "Wild Thing" keep kids motivated, and the clean, simple page layouts ensure their attention remains focused on one concept at a time.
00696449 Book/Online Audio $12.99

REFERENCE BOOKS

BASS SCALE FINDER
by Chad Johnson

Learn to use the entire fretboard with the *Bass Scale Finder*. This book contains over 1,300 scale diagrams for the most important 17 scale types.
00695781 6" x 9" Edition....................................... $7.99
00695778 9" x 12" Edition..................................... $7.99

BASS ARPEGGIO FINDER
by Chad Johnson

This extensive reference guide lays out over 1,300 arpeggio shapes. 28 different qualities are covered for each key, and each quality is presented in four different shapes.
00695817 6" x 9" Edition....................................... $7.99
00695816 9" x 12" Edition..................................... $7.99

MUSIC THEORY FOR BASSISTS
by Sean Malone

Acclaimed bassist and composer Sean Malone will explain the written language of music, using easy-to-understand terms and concepts, diagrams, and much more. The audio provides 96 tracks of examples, demonstrations, and play-alongs.
00695756 Book/Online Audio $17.99

STYLE BOOKS

BASS LICKS
by Ed Friedland

This comprehensive supplement to any bass method will help students learn over 200 great bass licks, lines and grooves in many rhythmic styles. *Bass Licks* illustrates how simple melodic patterns can become the springboard for group improvisation or the foundation of a song.
00696035 Book/Online Audio $14.99

BASS LINES
by Matt Scharfglass

500 expertly written bass lines, riffs and fills in a wide variety of musical genres are included in this comprehensive collection to help players expand their bass vocabulary. The examples cover many tempos, keys and feels, and include easy bass lines for beginners on up to advanced riffs for more experienced bassists.
00148194 Book/Online Audio $19.99

BLUES BASS
by Ed Friedland

Learn to play studying the songs of B.B. King, Stevie Ray Vaughan, Muddy Waters, Albert King, the Allman Brothers, T-Bone Walker, and many more. Learn riffs from blues classics including: Born Under a Bad Sign • Hideaway • Hoochie Coochie Man • Killing Floor • Pride and Joy • Sweet Home Chicago • The Thrill Is Gone • and more.
00695870 Book/Online Audio $14.99

COUNTRY BASS
by Glenn Letsch

21 songs, including: Act Naturally • Boot Scootin' Boogie • Crazy • Honky Tonk Man • Love You Out Loud • Luckenbach, Texas (Back to the Basics of Love) • No One Else on Earth • Ring of Fire • Southern Nights • Streets of Bakersfield • Whose Bed Have Your Boots Been Under? • and more.
00695928 Book/Online Audio $17.99

FRETLESS BASS
by Chris Kringel

18 songs, including: Bad Love • Continuum • Even Flow • Everytime You Go Away • Hocus Pocus • I Could Die for You • Jelly Roll • King of Pain • Kiss of Life • Lady in Red • Tears in Heaven • Very Early • What I Am • White Room • more.
00695850.. $19.99

FUNK BASS
by Chris Kringel

This is your complete guide to learning the basics of grooving and soloing funk bass. Songs include: Can't Stop • I'll Take You There • Let's Groove • Stay • What Is Hip • and more.
00695792 Book/Online Audio.............................. $22.99

R&B BASS
by Glenn Letsch

This book/audio pack uses actual classic R&B, Motown, soul and funk songs to teach you how to groove in the style of James Jamerson, Bootsy Collins, Bob Babbitt, and many others. The 19 songs include: For Once in My Life • Knock on Wood • Mustang Sally • Respect • Soul Man • Stand by Me • and more.
00695823 Book/Online Audio $17.99

ROCK BASS
by Sean Malone

This book/audio pack uses songs from a myriad of rock genres to teach the key elements of rock bass. Includes: Another One Bites the Dust • Beast of Burden • Money • Roxanne • Smells like Teen Spirit • and more.
00695801 Book/Online Audio.............................. $21.99

SUPPLEMENTARY SONGBOOKS

These great songbooks correlate with Books 1-3 of the *Hal Leonard Bass Method*, giving students great songs to play while they're still learning! The audio tracks include great accompaniment and demo tracks.

EASY POP BASS LINES

20 great songs that students in Book 1 can master. Includes: Come as You Are • Crossfire • Great Balls of Fire • Imagine • Surfin' U.S.A. • Takin' Care of Business • Wild Thing • and more.
00695810 Book Only.. $9.99
00695809 Book/Online Audio.............................. $15.99

MORE EASY POP BASS LINES

20 great songs for Level 2 students. Includes: Bad, Bad Leroy Brown • Crazy Train • I Heard It Through the Grapevine • My Generation • Pride and Joy • Ramblin' Man • Summer of '69 • and more.
00695819 Book Only.. $12.99
00695818 Book/Online Audio.............................. $16.99

EVEN MORE EASY POP BASS LINES

20 great songs for Level 3 students, including: ABC • Another One Bites the Dust • Brick House • Come Together • Higher Ground • Iron Man • The Joker • Sweet Emotion • Under Pressure • more.
00695821 Book... $9.99
00695820 Book/Online Audio.............................. $16.99

Visit Hal Leonard online at
www.halleonard.com